Image credit : « image : Freepik.com ».
This cover was designed using resources from Freepik.com

What kind of drink can be bitter and sweet?

Reali-tea.

Why couldn't the couple get married at the library?

It was all booked up.

What do you call a naughty lamb dressed up like a skeleton for Halloween? Baaad to the bone.

How did the dad prank his daughter using fake dog poop on April Fools Day? He told her to look out for her new sham-poo in the shower.

Want to know why nurses like red crayons?

Sometimes they have to draw blood.

What did the air conditioner say when it met a celebrity?

I'm a big fan.

What would the Terminator be called in his retirement?

The Exterminator.

What was Sherlock Holmes' favorite protein source?

Mystery meat.

What did Tennessee?

The same thing as Arkansas.

What did the dryer say to the boring duvet cover that just got out of the washer? Don’t be such a wet blanket.

My wife asked me to go get
6 cans of Sprite from the
grocery store.
I realized when I got home
that I had picked 7 up.

Why was the cow such a
heartthrob on the farm?

He was a s-moo-th talker.

Why do bees have sticky hair?

Because they use a honeycomb.

What's a writer's favorite train station?

Penn Station.

Why do some couples go to the gym?

Because they want their relationship to work out.

What was said about the messy, angry man who was eating a can of Pringles?
He's got a chip on his shoulder.

What do you call an angry musician flipping someone off?

A song bird.

What's it called when kittens get stuck in a tree?

A cat-astrophe.

Did you hear about the kidnapping at school?

It's fine, he woke up.

What kind of shape may have been knighted?

Cir-cles.

How can you tell it's a dogwood tree?

By the bark.

Why is sand so optimistic?

It has a can-dune attitude.

My boss told me to have a good day, so I went home.

What part of the museum makes everyone sneeze?

The sta-tues.

Why did the man fall down the well?

Because he couldn't see that well.

What did the baker say when she won an award?

It was a piece of cake.

When does a joke become a dad joke?

When it becomes apparent.

Why couldn't the couple respond right away when looking at wedding venues?

They were engaged.

Why is Peter Pan always flying?

Because he Neverlands.

What is Marco's favorite clothing store?

Polo.

Which state has
the most streets?

Rhode Island.

What do you call it when a
lawyer takes a test early in
the morning?

A breakfast bar.

What do you call 26 letters that went for a swim?

Alphawetical.

What do frogs use to track their exercise?

Fit (rib)bits.

What's the name of a very polite, European body of water?

Merci.

What kind of cleaning product feels a lot of motivation in life?

All-purpose.

Why was the color green notoriously single?

It was always so jaded.

Where was the dripping coming from in the fridge?

The leeks.

I used to hate facial hair, but then it grew on me.

Why was the hockey player gifted a new cap?

He was known for his hat tricks.

I want to make a brief joke, but it's a little cheesy.

What vegetable is kind to everyone?

The sweet potato.

Why did the coach go to the bank?

To get his quarterback.

How was the handsome runner described?

Dashing.

How do celebrities stay cool?

They have many fans.

What animals are the best to call if you get locked out of your house?

Monkeys.

What did the flowers do when the bride walked down the aisle?
They rose.

What did the geometry teacher say when the class had trouble solving a problem?
Let's try a different angle.

It takes guts to be
an organ donor.

Why don't phones ever go
hungry?

They have plenty of apps to
choose from.

What does Rockin' Robin do when she's bored?

Tweet.

Why couldn't the family leave the room after playing with Legos?

They were blocked.

I lost my job at the bank on my first day. A woman asked me to check her balance, so I pushed her over.

What makes a basketball court trendy and accessorized?

The hoops.

How do you row a canoe filled with puppies?

Bring out the doggy paddle.

What did the sapphire's best friend tell her?

You're a real gem.

Singing in the shower is fun until you get soap in your mouth. Then it becomes a soap opera.

I'm afraid for the calendar. Its days are numbered.

Why were the utensils stuck together?

They were spooning.

My wife said I should do lunges to stay in shape. That would be a big step forward.

What's a crafty dancer's favorite hobby?

Cutting a rug.

Why do fathers take an extra pair of socks when they go golfing?
In case they get a hole in one!

How does a penguin build his house?

Igloos it together.

Singing in the shower is fun until you get soap in your mouth. Then it's a soap opera.

What kind of music do chiropractors like?

Hip pop.

What do a tick and the Eiffel Tower have in common?

They're both Paris sites.

What kind of shoes does a lazy person wear?

Loafers.

What do you call a fish wearing a bowtie?

Sofishticated.

Why is cold water
so insecure?
Because it's never
called hot.

How do you follow Will
Smith in the snow?

You follow the fresh prints.

I was going to tell a time-traveling joke, but you guys didn't like it.

If April showers bring May flowers, what do May flowers bring?

Pilgrims.

Shouldn't the roof of your mouth actually be called the ceiling?

I thought the dryer was shrinking my clothes. Turns out it was the refrigerator all along.

Stop looking for the perfect match...use a lighter.

What do you call a factory that makes okay products?

A satisfactory.

I told my doctor I heard buzzing, but he said it's just a bug going around.

Dear Math, grow up and solve your own problems.

What kind of car does a sheep like to drive?

A lamborghini.

What did the janitor say when he jumped out of the closet?

Supplies!

What did the accountant say while auditing a document?
This is taxing.

Have you heard about the chocolate record player?

It sounds pretty sweet.

What did the two pieces of bread say on their wedding day?

It was loaf at first sight.

What did the ocean say to the beach?

Nothing, it just waved.

If the early bird gets the worm, I'll sleep in until there's pancakes.

Why do seagulls fly over the ocean? Because if they flew over the bay, we'd call them bagels.

Why do melons have weddings?

Because they cantaloupe.

I only know 25 letters of the alphabet. I don't know y.

I signed up for a marathon, but how will I know if it's the real deal or just a run through?

How does the moon cut his hair?

Eclipse it.

When you have a bladder infection, urine trouble.

What did one wall say to the other?

I'll meet you at the corner.

What did the drummer call his twin daughters?

Anna One, Anna Two!

What did the zero say to the eight?

That belt looks good on you.

What did the juicer say to the orange during self-quarantine?

Can’t wait to squeeze you!

A skeleton walks into a bar and says, ‘Hey, bartender. I’ll have one beer and a mop.’

What do you call a toothless bear?

A gummy bear!

Where do fruits go on vacation?

Pear-is!

Want to hear a joke about construction?

I'm still working on it.

I asked my dog what's two minus two. He said nothing.

That's a novel concept.

What did Baby Corn say to Mama Corn?

Where's Pop Corn?

Two goldfish are in a tank.

One says to the other: "Do you know how to drive this thing?"

What's the best thing about Switzerland?

I don't know, but the flag is a big plus.

What's Forrest Gump's password?

1forrest1

What does a sprinter eat before a race?

Nothing, they fast!

I tell dad jokes, but I don't have any kids. I'm a faux pa.

Where do you learn to make a banana split?

Sundae school.

What does a nosey pepper do?

It gets jalapeño business.

What has more letters than the alphabet?

The post office!

If a child refuses to nap, are they guilty of resisting a rest?

Dad, did you get a haircut?

No, I got them all cut!

Why do dads feel the need to tell such bad jokes? They just want to help you become a groan up.

What do you call a poor Santa Claus?

St. Nickel-less.

I know a lot of jokes about retired people, but none of them work.

I got carded at a liquor store, and my Blockbuster card accidentally fell out. The cashier said never mind.

Why are spiders so smart?

They can find everything on the web.

Where do boats go when they're sick?

To the boat doc.

RIP boiled water—you will be mist.

I don't trust those trees. They seem kind of shady.

What do you call two octopuses that look the same?

Itenticle.

My wife is really mad at the fact that I have no sense of direction. So I packed up my stuff and right!

What has one head, one foot, and four legs?

A bed.

How do you get a squirrel to like you?

Act like a nut.

Sore throats are a pain in the neck.

Why don't eggs tell jokes?

They'd crack each other up.

What does a house wear?

Address.

I don't trust stairs. They're always up to something.

Why did the scarecrow win an award?

He was out standing in his field.

What do you call someone with no body and no nose?

Nobody knows.

What's red and smells like blue paint?

Red paint.

Did you hear the rumor about butter?

Well, I'm not going to spread it!

My son asked me to put his shoes on, but I don't think they'll fit me.

Why couldn't the bicycle stand up by itself?

It was two tired.

I’ve been bored recently, so I decided to take up fencing.
The neighbors keep demanding that I put it

What did one hat say to the other?
Stay here! I’m going on ahead.

What do you call an unpredictable camera?

A loose Canon.

Why did Billy get fired from the banana factory?

He kept throwing away the bent ones.

I didn't get a haircut, I got them all cut.

Dad, can you put my shoes on?

No, I don't think they'll fit me.

Which U.S. state is known for its especially small soft drinks?

Minnesota.

Why can't a nose be 12 inches long?

Because then it would be a foot.

What do sprinters eat before a race?

Nothing—they fast.

What does a lemon say when it answers the phone?

Yellow!

What did one Dorito farmer say to the other?

Cool Ranch!

This graveyard looks overcrowded. People must be dying to get in.

Why couldn't the bicycle stand up by itself?

It was two-tired.

What kind of car does an egg drive?

A yolkswagen.

I'm so good at sleeping, I can do it with my eyes closed.

Dad, can you put the cat out?

I didn't know it was on fire.

People are usually shocked that I have a Police record. But I love their greatest hits!

How do you make 7 even?

Take away the s.

I told my girlfriend she drew on her eyebrows too high. She seemed surprised.

How does a taco say grace?

Lettuce pray.

What do you call a fibbing cat?

A lion.

What time did the man go to the dentist?

Tooth hurt-y.

Why shouldn't you write with a broken pencil?

Because it's pointless.

Why didn't the skeleton climb the mountain? It didn't have the guts.

I like telling Dad jokes...sometimes he laughs.

What do you call it when a snowman throws a tantrum?

A meltdown.

How do you
weigh a millennial?

In Instagrams.

How many tickles does it
take to make an octopus
laugh?

Ten tickles.

The wedding was so beautiful, even the cake was in tiers.

I have a joke about chemistry, but I don't think it will get a reaction.

What's the most patriotic sport?

Flag football.

What concert costs just 45 cents?

50 Cent featuring Nickelback!

Why were spectators confused by the koala's self-portrait?

It was bear.

What does a bee use to brush its hair?

A honeycomb!

Why did the envelope take so long to get ready?

It had to get addressed.

How do you make a tissue dance?

You put a little boogie in it.

What does a karate master get rewarded with while driving?

A seat belt.

Why did the math book look so sad?

Because of all of its problems!

What did the husband say to his wife right after getting LASIK surgery?
Aren't you a sight for sore eyes?

What do you call cheese that isn't yours?

Nacho cheese.

What do lions use
to look at their manes?

Mirroars.

My dad told me a joke
about boxing. I guess I
missed the punch line.

What did the dad say when his golden retriever was caught eating a hot dog?
It's a dog eat dog world out there.

What kind of shoes do ninjas wear?

Sneakers!

Do mascara and lipstick ever argue?

Sure, but then they makeup.

How does a penguin build its house?

Igloos it together.

What piece on the playground is always exhausted?

The tire swing.

How did Harry Potter get down the hill?

Walking. JK! Rowling.

Why did two tall people get along so well?

The could really see eye to eye.

I used to be addicted to soap, but I'm clean now.

Why was the gossip disliked at the coffee shop?

She always spilled the tea.

A guy walks into a bar...and he was disqualified from the limbo contest.

What does a writer have in common with a football player?

Anxiety over a rough draft.

You think swimming with sharks is expensive?

Swimming with sharks cost me an arm and a leg.

Where do wasps like to get lunch?

A bee-stro.

When two vegans get in an argument, is it still called a beef?

Why would doors do well on social media?

Everyone looks for their handles.

I ordered a chicken and an egg from Amazon. I'll let you know...

Which bathroom appliance would be the worst life preserver?

The sink.

Do you wanna box for your leftovers?

No, but I'll wrestle you for them.

Why was the dad sitting on a pack of playing cards?

His kid asked him to sit on the deck.

That car looks nice but the muffler seems exhausted.

What kind of bird is always getting hurt?

The owl.

Shout out to my fingers. I can count on all of them.

What's either a really gross animal issue OR an impressive, magical school?

Hogwarts.

If a child refuses to nap, are they guilty of resisting a rest?

What did the dishwasher say to the oven after a productive day?

You’ve been on fire!

What country’s capital is growing the fastest?

Ireland. Every day it’s Dublin.

Why did the cashier rip money in half?

They were asked to break a bill.

I once had a dream I was floating in an ocean of orange soda. It was more of a fanta sea.

What did one furniture maker say to another during a tense discussion?

Let's table this.

Did you know corduroy pillows are in style?

They're making headlines.

Why was the ghost so tired?

He worked the graveyard shift.

Did you hear about the kidnapping at school?

It's okay, he woke up.

Why do pancakes always win at baseball?

They have the best batter.

A cheeseburger walks into a bar. The bartender says, 'Sorry, we don't serve food here.'

www.ingramcontent.com/pod-product-compliance
Lightning Source LLC
LaVergne TN
LVHW012114160826
845678LV00014B/3085

* 9 7 9 8 8 4 6 3 6 5 5 9 9 *